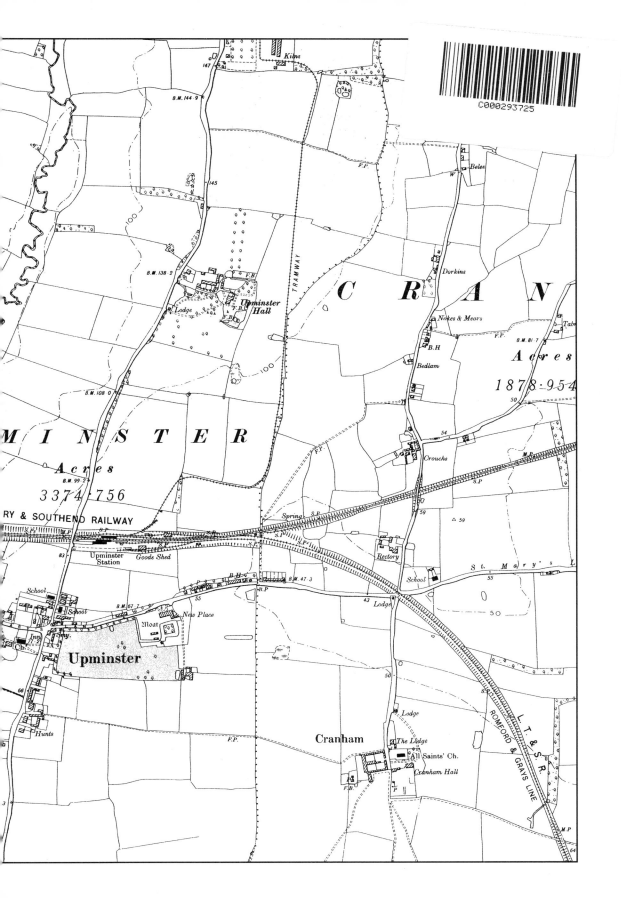

HORNCHURCH
& UPMINSTER

A Pictorial History

Over 2,000 years of history are encompassed by this aerial view of Hornchurch, photographed just before the Second World War. At the lower right section the buildings have been cleared from the old brewery site. In the centre, like a bull's-eye, the ancient *Britannia Inn* and its adjacent structure on the corner of High Street and North Street have also been demolished. The bow-shaped bend in the High Street remains and this is probably a very ancient feature. Hostelries for travellers probably stood at key points such as the corner of North Street west and on the *White Hart* (now the Madison Exchange) site, by the entrance into Station Lane. In between there was, in medieval times, an informal market for leather goods and other items. When Romford's market gained royal approval in 1247 the one at Hornchurch probably declined.

HORNCHURCH & UPMINSTER
A Pictorial History

Brian Evans

Phillimore

1996

Published by
PHILLIMORE & CO. LTD.
Shopwyke Manor Barn, Chichester, West Sussex

ISBN 1 86077 029 0

Printed and bound in Great Britain by
BIDDLES LTD.
Guildford, Surrey

List of Illustrations

Frontispiece: Aerial view of Hornchurch, *c.*1938

Front and Rear endpapers: The two villages: Ordnance Survey Map (1896).

Acknowledgements

The author would like to thank Mr. and Mrs. L.J. Brown, Mr. C. Edwards, Mr. Roy Squire and Mr. F.W.H. White, for their help with the illustrations in this volume, and Mr. Owen Routledge and Mr. Peter Watt for supplying invaluable information.

All those who have followed them also have been indebted to Hornchurch's historian C.T. Perfect and Upminster's chronicler T.L. Wilson. Thanks are also due to the London Borough of Havering Reference and Information Library.

HORNCHURCH: Its Ancient Origins

It seems that from pre-Roman times Hornchurch was a significant destination on a road that led from Ilford. Both Hornchurch and Ilford appear to have had a religious importance dating from before the Christian era. Everywhere in Britain we find that Christian churches and traditions took over the old sites of the pagan religions and made them their own. Often remnants of the old ways remained as part of the new and in Hornchurch's case the symbol of the bull's head placed at the east end of the church was a relic of an older religion. It is the only example of such a symbol on a church in the whole country.

A continuation of the ancient Ilford-Hornchurch Road, which is still at the Ilford end known as Green Lane (a name often denoting the antiquity of the route), leads to Upminster, Cranham and, curiously, Horndon. This hilltop village itself had its attractions for ancient peoples both through its comprehensive views over surrounding countryside and the mystery that resides in a hilltop site. The symbol of the horns may have been the symbol of the local leader 'Horn'—Horndon being the (fortified) hill of Horn the chieftain, around whom a personality cult or religion might have grown. Hornchurch, further along the ancient route on its little hill, also carried the symbol representing both leadership and religious worship in an age when daily life had a unity difficult for us today to understand. The persistence of ancient names in Essex is remarkable and a record of the heathen worship of Thunor and Woden exists in the names, for instance, of Thundersley near the Thames and Weeley (place of idol worship).

These names sometimes lasted through a period of time when there were no written traditions into the age of documentation where they surfaced after a different name had been used. Hornchurch is first known in the records as 'Ecclesia de Haveringis' or church of Havering—the royal manor of which it had become the capital—in 1163. This church was granted in that year as a further endowment to the Austin Canons or monks of St Nicholas and St Bernard, Montjoux. Henry II is supposed already to have granted an annual income of no less than £33 to these monks from the high Savoy in gratitude for help given to English travellers to Rome while crossing the mountain passes near the mother hospital of St Bernard. Documents of the Hornchurch daughter house began to display the Bull's Head emblem adopted by this house from a pagan predecessor, both in the Savoy and at Hornchurch. The bull had an added significance in that there existed in medieval times a flourishing leather industry at Hornchurch. The main High Street as it later became was then known as Pallestrate (1288), Pelstrate (1280s-1370s), from an origin which is similar to our 'pelt' meaning a skin or hide, showing the importance of the leather preparation/ tanning industry in Hornchurch in the Middle Ages. When road conditions at the time caused very slow journeys to other places in the region some hides may have been exported by the Ingrebourne waterway of the time—the loaders of the boats processing down what was then known as Hythelane (in a document of 1497) to the quay or landing place. Along Lychelane (in documents of 1411 and 1503) corpses would have been carried for burial in Hornchurch churchyard—the way extending along the fields from Romford which did not have the right of burial until 1410. Until this date Hornchurch was the main centre for religious activity in the area. Six documents between 1308 and 1395 in a collection at Oriel College, Oxford mention the Hornchurch Road from Ilford and London and in them it is described variously as 'the King's way leading from Ilford to Hornminster', 'the King's highway ...', 'the King's street' and 'the public road ...' showing it as having become a high profile route in the days when there was a royal palace at Havering-atte-Bower village. Most of our roads were then mere tracks, footways, cattle-drovers' routes or non-existent. Businessmen and courtiers followed in the royal wake and the Hornchurch of the time must have been a prosperous and active place. The monks of Hornchurch, no less than their colleagues in the high mountains of Savoy, had a role and a duty to succour poor travellers. To this end they set up places where travellers could find refreshment and temporary rest and shelter. The advent of pilgrims passing through the area on their way to cross the Thames to the shrine of St Thomas à Becket increased the demand and at least two sites in Hornchurch village may have been used—what was later the *Britannia Inn* on the corner of North Street and High Street and the *White Hart* at the bottom of Church Hill (now the Madison Exchange).

1 Hornchurch Church on its hilltop stands framed by trees, 1813. It is described at this time as 'a spacious stone structure, with clerestory windows; it consists of three chancels and a nave, which is separated from the north and south aisles by arches supported by pillars. At the west end of the church is a gallery. The tower contains six bells, and is about 86 feet high ...'. In 1802 it had undergone a thorough repair at a cost of almost £2,000 (then, of course, a considerable sum of money).

2 The fields the monks knew well. This view from the north with St Andrew's, on the horizon, emphasises the continuing rurality of Hornchurch's surroundings, even at the beginning of the 20th century. The Chaplaincy can be seen on the left in the distance and the buildings of Hornchurch Hall on the right, both from the rear. A wall divides the Hall and Chaplaincy (in 1915 still known as the Vicarage)—the wall being part of the adaptation from priory to parochial use.

3 The roofline of the Chaplaincy, 1915. Part of the medieval framework of this building came to light after demolition began in 1970. A fire started by vandals while it was derelict revealed important remains of the west wing or Solar Hall—part of the house built in 1399-1400 on the site of the Hornchurch Priory. Apart from this wing, the house had been rebuilt in the late 17th century as a two-storey timber-framed structure.

4a Impression of the monks of St Bernard at Hornchurch by P.C. Haydon Bacon.

4b The St Bernard Hospice in Switzerland, early 20th-century.

It may seem strange that a foreign priory and monks should be established in England but it should be remembered that the church was then truly international. King Henry III endowed this sub-priory in England partly to thank the mother house for its hospitality to English travellers and perhaps partly to use their expertise in helping pilgrims here on their way to shrines in England and abroad (part of an international network—nobody else in these early days would willingly help travellers).

4c An early 20th-century view of the St Bernard Hospice in Switzerland.

A GOOD NAME ENDURETH

4d The Bull's Head from the priory seal incorporated in the arms of Hornchurch Urban District.

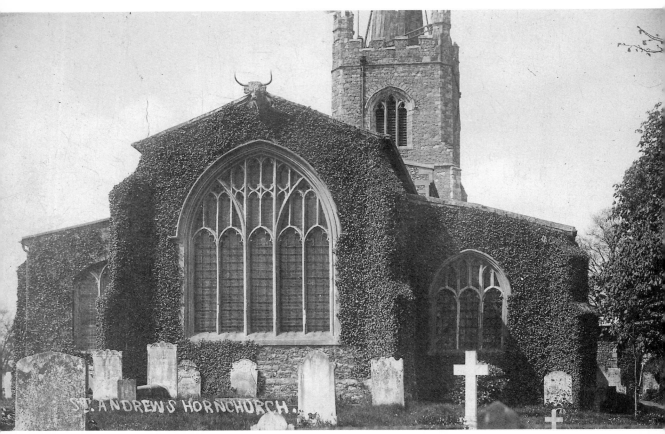

ST. ANDREWS HORNCHURCH.

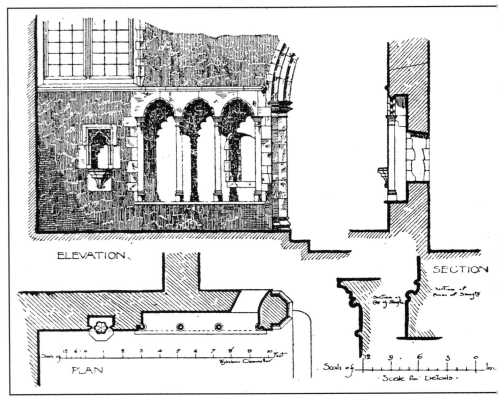

ELEVATION.

SECTION

PLAN

Scale of Details.

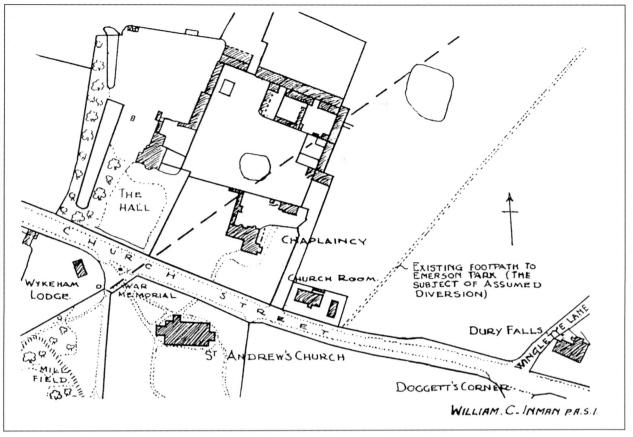

THE HALL

WYKEHAM LODGE.

WAR MEMORIAL

CHAPLAINCY

CHURCH ROOM.

CHURCH STREET

St ANDREW'S CHURCH

MILL FIELD.

DOGGETT'S CORNER.

EXISTING FOOTPATH TO EMERSON PARK (THE SUBJECT OF ASSUMED DIVERSION)

DURY FALLS

WANGLETTE LANE

WILLIAM. C. INMAN P.A.S.I.

5 (*above left*) The east end of St Andrew's about 1900, with the unique bull's head and horns at the apex. It still speaks to us today from the mists of early history. Was this the device of Horn, an early local religious and political leader?

7 (*above*) Plan of the Church and Chaplaincy area in about 1920. The dashed line across the upper part shows the line of the assumed original path through the Priory Court. The lower dotted line shows a later diversion of this path, after the monks had departed and the Chaplaincy was built, on the site of former priory buildings.

6 (*left*) The triple sedilia (stone seats for priests) and piscina (stone water basin) in St Andrew's chancel. The sedilia are of the same date as the nave arcades, early English period of the 13th century, but have been restored since they were discovered in the 1871 restoration of the church. A hagioscope or viewing window pierces the westernmost arcade of the sedilia. This allowed church officials to be aware of the progress of ceremonies in the chancel.

The stone coffin lid, the oldest memorial in St Andrew's, believed to be that of an early prior. It was found buried in the nave during the alterations of 1871. The cross carved on it has been described as 'of simple and unusual but elegant design, with an orb on the shaft, just below the head'.

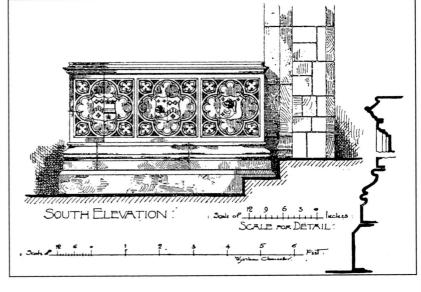

8 Brass in St Andrew's in memory of Thomas Hone and his family, 1604. Thomas was one of Hornchurch's country gentlemen who valued the peace of the village and its surrounding fields as a rest from the stress of business and court life in London. The Latin motto translates as 'Let us walk honestly as in the day'. His estate, Carolens, is thought to be Lees Gardens, a Hornchurch manor listed in Morant's *Essex*. Thomas wears a long gown with large spirally-striped false sleeves. The lady is attired very plainly in French bonnet, neck ruff and a plain over-gown, enormously set off at the hips—a style of the time. The children are dressed similarly, although the sons wear short cloaks—a fashion post-dating their father's.

9 Tomb of a great man. The inscription on a brass plate—the original having disappeared—read, 'Off yo charite py for the soule of Willm Ayloffe, gentylman owner of the mano of Bretensse yn the County of Essex ...'. The Ayloffe family played an active part in the history of the county for about three centuries, owning large estates and acting as High Sherriff of Essex. They were loyal supporters of the Stuart kings and sat as Knights of the Shire in the first Parliament after Charles II's Restoration. They were also eminent in law. The last baronet became an antiquary and archaeologist of note. William married Audrey, daughter of Sir John Shaw, Alderman of London, and had two sons, William and Thomas.

10 An early photograph of Bretons Manor House, also known as Brittons. This early view, though affected by its age, hints at the lost splendours of its past. Remarkably the house still stands and the Borough of Havering have restored the fine railings at the front. At this date in the late 19th century the house was still rather isolated in a wide expanse of marsh and farmland. In the reign of Henry VII Bretons was purchased by William Ayloffe who came from a distinguished family of Saxon extraction, originally based in the county of Kent. In the reign of Edward IV the estate had belonged to the Scargill family, one of whom was appointed Keeper of Havering Park.

11 A view of Hornchurch Mill, 1910. A reference to a mill in the Mill field in 1262 is evidence for the antiquity of milling on this site. There are records of various re-buildings. Apart from New College in 1494, other lessees were members of the Legatt family; William had it rebuilt in 1564 and John in his will of 1607 devised it to his son Thomas. The mill ceased grinding in 1912 and it burnt down in 1921. The timber-framed Mill Cottage, apparently of 17th-century origin with early 19th-century alterations, survives.

12a Pilgrim Ways. Pilgrims sitting round a communal table for a meal. On pilgrimages to the shrine of St Thomas at Canterbury they streamed down the lanes of Hornchurch, choosing the village because it provided a hostel, originally run by the monks where they could find food and shelter.

12b Wingletye Lane may have been a favourite north to south route from Brentwood where the remains of St Thomas's Chapel still can be seen. In this picture, although the 20th century has brought houses, the old lane with its hedges and surrounding fields is fairly unchanged from the track the pilgrims knew.

TREASURE TROVE INQUEST

AT HORNCHURCH

PROCEDURE THAT HAS ENDURED 1,000 YEARS

448 SILVER COINS FOUND

TWO FORGERIES OF REIGN OF HENRY III

"This is one of the rare occasions when I have to exercise a pleasant function, " said Mr. L. F. Beccle, the Coroner, when he held an inquest at Hornchurch on Saturday morning on treasure trove.

The inquest, which aroused considerable local interest, was on 448 silver coins of the reign of Henry III which were unearthed by Council workmen when excavating in Upminster-road at a point 50 feet east of the Parish Church. Mr. W. C. Allen, Clerk to Hornchurch Council, had identified the coins as of great antiquity and reported the matter to the Coroner who intimated that he would hold an inquest into the find.

CORONER DEFINES TREASURE TROVE

A jury was empanelled, and addressing the jury at the outset, the Coroner said that was one of the rare occasions when he had to exercise a pleasant function. It was an inquiry into treasure trove, but it was necessary that he should first define treasure trove. The best definition that he could find was that treasure trove was where any gold or silver in coin, plate or bullion was found concealed in a house or in the earth or in a private place the owner therof being unknown, in which case the treasure belonged to the King or his grantee, having the franchise of treasure trove. "But if he that laid it be known, or afterwards discovered, the owner and not the King is entitled to it, this prerogative right only applying in the absence of the owner to claim the property."

The Coroner added that the crux of the matter was that it was the hiding of the property and not the abandoning of it that entitled the King to it. If the property was thrown away on the ground or a public place or any other similar way the first finder was entitled to it. But if the property was concealed in one way or another that gave the King the right of possession and ownership ...

search of the site was made. It was excavated down to the original gravel bed but only a few more single coins were found. He subsequently took the coins to the British Museum where he was informed that they were mainly of the reign of Henry III and were probably buried between 1250 and 1260. Among them were some rarer coins known as the 'short cross' which were withdrawn from circulation when the long cross coins were issued.

There were also 17 coins of the reign of Alexander III of Scotland, who reigned between 1249 and 1285. There were two different sorts of these coins with the heads showing in the opposite way. They were products of the Edinburgh mint. There were also several Irish coins of the Dublin mint.

TWO FORGERIES

"Curiously enough," said Mr. Allen, "there are two forgeries, one of which broke when I picked it up, being copper covered with silver, and the other is of an alloy of some sort."

The Coroner: So there were coiners even in those days.

Mr. Allen: The forgery is not a good one. There are definite differences in it.

The Coroner: Probably Scotland Yard wasn't so active then. (Laughter.)

Thus, said Mr. Allen, there were 449 intact coins, one a forgery.

The Coroner: That is not "treasure".

QUESTIONS FOR JURY

The Coroner said that was all the evidence that would be called and he would proceed to put the questions to the jury.

The questions and answers were:—

What did the find consist of?—448 silver coins

Where was the find deposited?—In Upminster-road, Hornchurch, 50 feet to the east of the parish church.

Were they intentionally hidden or accidentally lost, or purposely abandoned?—They were intentionally concealed.

Are you statisfied that the owner is unknown?-Yes.

Did the finder or finders conceal their find?—No.

Mr. Allen said there used to be a hedge on both sides of the road, but owing to building development the Council took in a portion of the adjoining land into the highway and the site on which the find was made was part of the land which had been brought into the highway. It was previously behind the line of the hedge.

He said he claimed to be the finder of 67 coins, because he desired that after the Crown and the British Museum had done with them, that some should come back and become ...

---

13 In August 1938 great interest was created in the district by the discovery, 18 inches under the soil of the roadway opposite Hornchurch Church, of a cache of silver coins from the Middle Ages. This hoard was disturbed by the pickaxe of a council worker in the midst of paving works. Four hundred and forty-eight pennies of the reign of Henry III were uncovered. They included 17 coins of the Scottish King Alexander III and about twelve Irish. Henry and Alexander were both reinstaters of the purity of their kingdom's coinage and it is from Henry's time that the word sterling as in pound sterling comes. He created a new coinage of sterling or standard weight to replace previous debased issues. A treasure trove inquest was held locally and the coins were declared crown property. The original find-spot was within the grounds of the former priory and the coins therefore may have been the property of the almoner who received gifts from the rich and dispensed alms to the poor.

14a Detail of William of Wykeham from the magnificent tomb at Winchester Cathedral. He was twice Chancellor of England as well as Bishop of Winchester. When the monks were sent out of England Wykeham pounced and got control of their lands, estates and the rents. About 1391 William obtained permission from the Pope and from King Richard II to purchase them so that he could endow his New College at Oxford which he had built between 1379 and 1387. He paid 4,000 English gold nobles and 500 French francs. For over 600 years the Warden and Fellows of New College have had this connection with Hornchurch, appointing over forty vicars temporal or chaplains to St Andrew's in that time.

14b There is also a connection between the muniment tower of New College and the tower of St Andrew's, seen here about 1896. It is believed that Wykeham was responsible for their design. There are effigies of Wykeham at each, both showing the Bishop in the act of blessing his flock. In later years the tower became a landmark visible to shipping on the Thames and contributions towards its repair are said to have been made by Trinity House.

15 Suttons House about 1914. The Manor formed part of the lands and estates granted to Hornchurch Priory or the Hostel of St Bernard. The old manor house a mile south of the village went long ago and this fairly modern house replaced it. Farmer Tom Crawford farmed the land around from 1888 until 1933, although part of it was used as a First World War airfield. In the original grant to the Priory in 1158 this estate was worth £25.

Down the Ancient High Street and Beyond

16 A summer day on Church Hill, Hornchurch, facing east, *c*.1908. All these buildings behind the *White Hart* have been replaced by wide pavements, except the *King's Head* and the Chalice building beyond (in the centre distance). Opposite them looms the Old Hornchurch Brewery wall which enclosed the working buildings and a domestic structure, seen here just inside the front wall, and the hoist room projecting over the pavement at right centre. Ainsworth's cycle makers on the right (later Rumsey's) and the shop opposite both have interesting exterior lamps.

17 A quiet day on Church Hill (now part of High Street) in 1914. The *King's Head* and its adjacent buildings include the Bottling Stores associated with the brewery which are through an archway below the *King's Head*. The 'sparkling bottled ales and nourishing stout' were produced at the manufactory opposite. The outside of the brewery can be seen on the right, sunk in shadow, though a high chimney is clearly visible along the frontage.

18 A 1960s view down Church Hill (now renamed High Street). Formerly the Brewery, the empty lot on the left faces a redecorated *King's Head*. Mac's Café occupies one of the 'Chalice' group of buildings which in recent years have been dated as partly 15th-century (a dividing wall) and also 17th-century although they have been altered on many occasions since. The roofline of the original building lay at right angles to the road—a common layout in earlier centuries.

19 The High Street in the 1950s from a *White Hart* vantage point. The property on the right, occupied by the Little Flower Shop, has not yet been demolished. On the left by the bus Aleys the Bakers (formerly Beards), a white building with a filled-in side window protrudes into the road—it will soon disappear for road-widening. This colour-washed brick structure dated from the 18th century with a very attractive bow window of the early 19th century. It came down in 1956.

20 This Essex weather-board group of buildings at the corner of North Street and High Street remained throughout the 1950s. The *Green Lantern* has occupied more than one site in Hornchurch at different times. Marshall's the Newsagents had previously been Smith's and before that Drake's in the same trade. The next shop had been Franklyn's, shoe repairers, keeping up Hornchurch's connection with leather.

21 The *Britannia Inn* building at the western corner of the High Street/North Street junction, 1909. No longer an inn, the building was used for various purposes including a café. The stonework in the chimney stack and the large stone fireplaces, uncovered when it was demolished in 1938 to make way for a Burton's chain tailors, indicate an ancient communal/ecclesiastical building. It seems likely that this was a travellers'/pilgrims' hostel provided by Hornchurch Priory brethren, of which there may have been more than one at different times. Cage Row is the group of buildings further up North Street—so-named from the village lock-up or prison on the other side of the road.

22 The bend in the High Street, in the late 1930s, looking east. The new *White Hart* building in the centre distance has recently been built (1935). A bottleneck still exists nearer the camera. The right-hand shop, which was known for years as Charlie Baker's the grocer's, has now become Green's stores, part of a chain. All the buildings beyond this are of venerable age and show how swiftly Hornchurch was to change in the next few decades for they were to be swept away when the road line was set back.

23 Moving westwards, away from the bend, the next shop to Charlie Baker's was once Gotts the Saddler, seen here on the left. He also occupied the very old building with the archway next to it going west. A later owner of this business, described as 'saddler, collar and harness maker' was George Beckett. These buildings were demolished in February 1937, a barn, shed and stables at the back having burnt down in a fire in July 1933. All of the area behind was a child's dream of a playground as behind the barn was an orchard and a meadow with a running brook below. The Archway buildings apparently dated as far back as the 15th and 16th centuries. What a tourist resort Hornchurch could have become if they had survived.

24 Westward again, we start to approach the *Bull Inn* area in the mid distance about 1908. It is a typical village day with carts going about their business and a window cleaner in the background. In the distance are the trees of the Grey Towers parkland which stretched from Ravensbourne Bridge to Billet Lane.

25 Near the *Bull Inn* about 1916, when Ind Coope's bitter was on sale at three-and-a-half old pennies per pint. There is a noticeable gradient in the road towards North Street corner.

26 Pulling down Appleton's Almshouses, 1967. These particular buildings dated back to 1838, although an earlier version had stood on the site in High Street, nearly opposite the *Bull*.

27 A contrast—modern commerce vies with the picturesque on the south side of High Street towards the Billet Lane junction in 1913. Moss Bros, Brooklands Farm Dairy was only one of many dairies in the district, Banyards of Nelmes Farm being one of the best known. Charles Evans later took over Moss's. Arthur Wakeham is the small family grocer's—a tiny business compared with the giant Sainsbury's that now serves Hornchurch just across the road.

28a & b Two winter views of the very old building facing Billet Lane shortly before demolition in 1960 together with its later neighbours as far as the *Cricketers' Inn* which has been rebuilt and set back, out of the picture.

29 Behind the tree, at the corner of Billet Lane, are the Pennants Almshouses seen here in the 1930s. They had been founded in 1590, converted into a workhouse in the 18th century and reconverted to almshouses in the 1830s. Sainsbury's now occupies the block.

HORNCHURCH. HIGH ST.

30 Standing more to the west, in 1925 the photographer has recorded a panorama of the High Street, full of incident, including a 'General' bus on Route 86 bowling along in the distance towards Upminster.

31 The west end of the High Street contained many small semi-detached 19th-century cottages, some of which are still there. They were representative of several others dotted about the village.
(*above*) Weather-board cottage decorated for an Edwardian carnival. Note the small sign outside the brick cottage identifying the occupier as a fireman serving as a contact for any outbreak in the area.
(*below*) Bratchell's Cottage, October 1973, with adjoining buildings.

32 The High Street end of North Street, 1905. The village schools on the right were built by subscription on land presented by New College, 1855. Both girls and infants were taught here whilst the boys occupied a small building opposite St Andrew's Church. Later, in 1902, a new building arose in what became Westland Avenue but was at the time only waste ground. Nearer to the camera on the left is the block of six cramped cottages known as Cage Row.

33 The Baptist Church and its adjoining buildings face the schools in North Street, 1920. The church remained until recent years when the site was re-developed and it moved upstairs in a modern unit.

34 (*top left*) In 1960 these old cottages still remained on what was to become the site for the new Hornchurch Library. A thaw has begun and the snow has melted, causing a quagmire on the site below on the right where the new fire station was soon to be built (opened July 1964).

35 (*above*) A narrow part of old Station Lane leading towards Hornchurch village and the *White Hart*, 1905.

36 (*left*) On the Hornchurch side of the narrow section the Victorian houses of Station Lane sweep in an arc towards the *White Hart*, which is behind the photographer. For the beginning of the 1930s the left-hand side of the road appears quite commercialised. Next door to the shops but out of sight in this picture was the Hornchurch Cinema, for which posters can be seen on the low hoarding. The cinema became the first site for the Queen's Theatre which took over the same building in 1953.

37 Pigs and piglets. Hornchurch was a truly rural place outside the village nucleus and even in 1912 a photographer was producing a series of country scenes of the surrounding fields.

38 An advert of 1830 for the sale of the live and dead stock from Lee Gardens Farm gives an insight into crops, livestock and farming equipment to be found on a local farming estate.

HORNCHURCH, ESSEX.

TO BE SOLD BY AUCTION,
BY W. DAWSON,

On Friday, Sept. 24, 1830, at Twelve o'Clock, on the Premises called Lee Gardens, near Hornchurch, by Order of H. T. JENKINS, Esq, who has left the Estate,

ALL the valuable LIVE and DEAD FARMING STOCK, GROWING CROPS, &c.; consisting of six acres of fine Shaw potatoes, six acres of real Quebec potatoes, and two acres of March champions; a fine stack of about 40 loads of prime meadow hay, the produce of about eight acres of second-cut clover, and a small stack of oats; a famous three-year-old bull, three fine milch cows, a sow, and nine store pigs, cart and nag horses and colts, and a handsome bay pony; farming implements, loading, market, and tumbrel carts, two light carts, neat dennet gig, two sets of harness, land rollers, and machines; large malt mill, barn utensils, and other valuable effects; which will appear in Catalogues to be had at the Bull and Red Lion Inns, Whitechapel; White Horse, Ilford; White Hart, Brentwood; at the Inns in the neighbourhood; on the Premises; and of the Auctioneer, Romford, Essex.

39 Appropriately for Hornchurch, the local cattle sport some fearsome-looking horns although the watching boy seems quite unperturbed as he too is photographed, 1912.

COUNTRY SCENE HORNCHURCH

40a & b The local fields were bisected by traditional rights of way. Some country people rarely trod the roads except from necessity. One of these paths has been summarily closed by the landowner. A deputation of prams is drawn up outside the gate apparently ready to challenge the owner's decision. The bridge is probably one spanning the Ravensbourne on the Grey Towers Estate.

41 'Absconded ... John Westwood.' This notice from an 1831 newspaper shows how parish councils, an earlier form of local government, tried to avoid having to pay for the maintenance of families who came from other parts and had become destitute.

ABSCONDED,

ABOUT TWELVE MONTHS SINCE,

And left his Family chargeable to the Parish of Hornchurch, in the County of Essex,

JOHN WESTWOOD, 35 years of age, light complexion, light hazel eyes, light hair, rather curled; about 5 feet 7 inches high; had on a black silk plush waistcoat, with dark fustian sleeves, corded trousers and jacket; is a native of Radley Green, near Blackmore; has been in the habit of travelling the country with a pony and cart, selling tapes, threads, &c. buying old rags, with the name of John Harris on the cart, and commonly called Jack Rags; was seen about Sudbury and Colchester.

Whoever will give information of the said John Westwood, shall receive FIVE GUINEAS REWARD and all reasonable expenses of his apprehension, by applying to the Overseers of Hornchurch.

May 27th, 1831.

42 Tap room at the old *Harrow Inn*, Hornchurch Road, 1879. The inn at this time was almost surrounded by fields and would be visited at the end of the day by local agricultural workers. The old building probably dated from the 17th century. It was a rambling affair lit by oil lamps. Water had to be obtained from a pump at the west end. In 1865 Philip Irving Brown was the licensee.

43 Several carts stand outside the new *Harrow*, rebuilt in the 1890s. At least one of the carts appears to be overloaded. It is difficult to date this picture as, although it seems to be before 1914, there is a curious aerial-like object in the garden on the right and the Ind Coope sign at the side is very weathered-looking.

44 The *Bridge House Inn* on the Hornchurch border with Upminster, 1908. There is an early record of a 'Brigge House', located here, in a document of 1373 (Edward III's reign). In medieval times there was a ford at the side of the bridge for use by more substantial vehicles: in 1617 it was described as a 'horse bridge' and in decay. The road up to Upminster, in early medieval days, was twice as wide which explains how there was room for a ford. This extra waste was gradually enclosed and houses were built on it.

Hornchurch
CHURCH.

The Parishioners are respectfully informed that the CHURCH, having undergone a thorough Repair, will be

RE-OPENED

for Divine Service on Sunday, the 12th of November, 1826.

Service to begin at 11 o'Clock in the Morning, and 3 o'Clock in the Afternoon.

C. HARVEY, PRINTER, ROMFORD.

45 During various periods of repair, older features of the church have surfaced. During the 10 weeks' closure in 1826 the medieval wall paintings discovered in 1802 were covered by a complete repainting of the interior together with a reopening and restoration of the east window and repair of the tower windows. The paintings which brightened up the interior in the Middle Ages included: Lazarus in a coffin with two angels and a large effigy of a bishop (chancel south wall); outlines of skeletons and a dragon (in the body of the church); a figure with a scroll above the head (in each of the sedilia brought to light in 1871); the Ayloffe arms (wooden screen between chancel/ north chapel).

46 Firemen and cart in the High Street about 1908. They are preparing to take part in the carnival. When Hornchurch became a parish council in 1894, it immediately took steps to create an effective fire brigade. A manual pump which required the services of 22 men to get it operating at its maximum rate was, after a while, brought from the brewery and placed in a shed close to where the first fire station was to be built in Billet Lane (now part of Sainsbury's car park).

47 Here we see the fire brigade outside the fire station built in 1907 in Billet Lane on land given to the council by Colonel Henry Holmes. Certain names of firemen have recurred in the records: Bratchell, Alabaster, Collin, Fry, Wall, Dorrington, Hurrell. The Chief Officer with the epaulettes, holding the young lad's hand, is E.G. Bratchell who succeeded the first Chief Officer, J. Wood, after only a few years and held the post for almost 30 years.

48 A practice drill for the benefit of members of the Parish Council Fire Brigade Committee to show off new items of equipment, before the First World War. Long before fire bells or telephone calls were installed in the volunteer firemen's homes, one method of summoning the men was to send a youngster out on a bicycle to blow a bugle at strategic points in the village. Many of the early fires were of course at farm premises. Mine host of the *Bull Inn* provided the first horses to pull the manual pump when a call-out came.

Hornchurch Cricket Club

In the late 18th and early 19th centuries Hornchurch fielded one of the most celebrated village cricket teams in England. These indeed were heady days, when enthusiasm for the game was at a height in the county and some neighbouring parts. Challenges were flung down and readily accepted with a gusto, harking back to medieval jousts and tournaments. The press notices of the day give us glimpses only of this activity:

1783 'Match to be played on Tuesday, August 26th at the Green Man, Navestock, Ingatestone v. Hornchurch for a guinea a man'. (This was Hornchurch's first season.)

1784 'On July 8th, at Hornchurch, Hornchurch v. Dartford with Mr. Booker, for £50 a side—wickets pitched at 9'.

Summer of 1784 'Hornchurch played Ingatestone at Corbets Tey'.

August 1784 'last Monday se'nnnight [i.e. week] a Match of Cricket was played at Knavestock in Essex by the United Clubs of Kennington & Bow against the Hornchurch Club, which was won with great ease by the latter.'

49 As Perfect mentions in his history, 'Early in the last century Hornchurch was one of the great cricketing centres of the county. There would appear to be little doubt that the celebrated pitch in Grey Towers Park was well over 100 years old when it was last played upon in 1914. Prior to 1876 ... the cricket field formed part of the estate of Langtons which at the time the Bearblock Eleven became famous, was owned by Mrs. Massu. In those days a cricket match at Hornchurch was an event of such importance that the forge hammers at Fairkytes Foundry ceased to beat and all the village kept high holiday ... on match days a string of carriages, brakes and drags reached all up and down the High Street from the *Cricketers' Inn* to the *White Hart Hotel* ... the spectators often numbered several thousands.' From 1918 to 1925 the ground was in Wingletye Lane and from 1925-44 in front of Fairkytes where the Queen's Theatre now stands.

HORNCHURCH AND MARY-LA-BONNE.—On Thursday, eleven of the Hornchurch Club played against a similar number of gentlemen belonging to the Mary-la-bonne Club, with Bayley and Cobbett, at Lord's ground. The play throughout was very good. The Hornchurch in their first innings got their runs very slowly, from the excellence of Cobbett and Bayley's round-arm bowling. At the close of the day's play, the score was as follows:—

MARY-LA-BONNE.

	FIRST INNINGS.		SECOND DO.
E. Ellis, Esq. b. out	0	run out	12
Bayley, do.	35	bowled out	0
Hon. S. D. Montagu, c. out	4	do. by Dow	9
Sir F. Bathurst, bow. out	1	do.	0
Cobbett, do.	8	do.	0
T. Grimstead, Esq. do.	10	run out	13
W. Bennett Esq. do.	5	caught out	2
Hon. F. Gordon, leg b. w.	1	b. by Stevens	2
T. Denne, Esq. bow. out	0	do.	6
T. C. Pack, Esq. not out	2	not out	2
Capt. Loftus, stumpt out	4	leg b. w.	12
Byes, &c.	1		0
	—71		—58

HORNCHURCH.

FIRST INNINGS.

Mr. Terry, bowled out	12
W. Bearblock, do.	2
C. Thompson, caught out	6
J. Stevens, bowled out	0
Adlam, do.	7
Dow, do.	0
John Bearblock, not out	14
Thompson, bowled out	2
West, caught out	5
P. Bearblock, bowled out	0
Stevens, caught out	11
Byes, &c.	2
	—61

Messrs. Adlam and John Bearblock went in for the second innings; but after the latter had scored five, the rain prevented the further progress of the match.—The return match will be played at Hornchurch in July.

CRICKET

THE RETURN MATCH between the SPRING-FIELD and HORNCHURCH CLUBS will be played in Springfield Lawn, on TUESDAY NEXT, the 5th of August.

50 Park Lane School, north-west Hornchurch, Class No.1, *c.*1910. From the middle of the 19th century, the nation became aware of the importance of education and Hornchurch shared in the benefits of more knowledge for all.

51 The Cottage Homes, Hornchurch Road.

Thousands of children came through these gates in quest of a better life. The homes were set up by the Shoreditch parish guardians in 1889. They accommodated the inner city children who had become wards of the state 'through the misfortunes of their parents' often because they had become destitute in the days before the welfare state. The idea was to create a self-contained village and the children, after a fortnight's assessment in the Lodge near the gates, were sent to one of the Cottages and placed under the care of houseparents. Up until the First World War all the children went to the school in the homes, but at some later date groups began to be sent to various local schools, perhaps in order to begin to integrate them into the local community.

52 Ivy Cottage. Mr. and Mrs. H.E. Steed were Superintendent and Matron around 1913.

53 The Home had its own hospital or infirmary where sick children were treated. In 1917 it was in the charge of Miss K. Willis and dealt with an average of 20 in-patients mostly, presumably, suffering from common childhood illnesses some of the youngsters may have arrived at St Leonard's in a run-down state due to poor conditions in their former homes. The well-equipped infirmary was also dealing with 80 out-patients daily for 'minor ills'.

54 An air-view of St Leonard's, *c.*1930. Hornchurch Bus Garage has recently been built to the west on the main road together with some housing development. Most of the area around the homes however is still occupied by fields. In 1917 there were 13 cottages each trying to reproduce the atmosphere of a true home, albeit a large family one. In those set apart for big boys there were man-and-wife teams as foster parents. The girls were separately housed under the care of a foster mother, assisted by the elder girls who thus learned the principles of looking after a home.

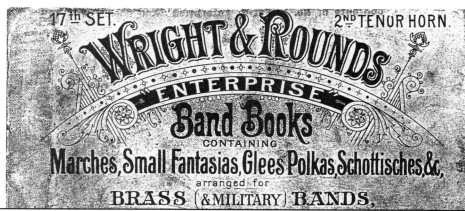

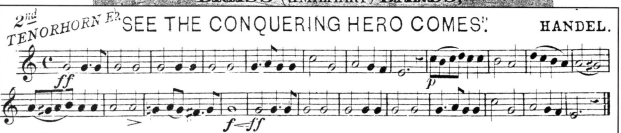

55 'See the Conquering Hero ...'. Band book from St Leonard's. One of the specialised occupations and courses of instruction was musical study. A boys' band with some forty youngsters regularly in training was under the direction of Mr. H. W. Alden in 1917. Musical entertainment was provided by the boys inside and outside the Homes. Many left to join military bands as an occupation. Bakery, gardening, shoemaking, decorating, tailoring and carpentry were also taught to the boys while the girls learned cookery, laundry work, needlework and general domestic economy. The homes are now the site of a private housing development, some of the original buildings are being preserved.

56a Carnival fun about 1909. Decorated bicycles were all the rage.

56b The Dotty Band appears to have been a standard feature of Hornchurch with its musical traditions dating back over the centuries—heralds and trumpeters accompanying royalty on their early visits—A primitive band in the church—the bandsmen of the Cottage Homes and today's marching bands (often mostly female).

56c A highly decorated version of the Fairlop Boat showing how inventive carnivals used to be in aid of a good cause, often the local hospital.

57 The proud musicians of the Hornchurch Village Band line up in front of an ivy-clad house in 1910.

58 On a less formal occasion the band proceeds across Emerson Park station bridge in their ordinary clothes. Perhaps this is a practice march for some later event. The fine day has ensured a good turnout of relatives and spectators.

59 This First World War view of the same bridge, facing in the opposite direction. Emerson Park station entrance on the left and a newspaper kiosk run by A. Smith whose shop is in the High Street. *The Chequers* replaced an antique version about 1899 which had an old red tiled roof and very ancient appearance. Butts Green starts here and was probably the spot where the young men of the medieval village came to practise their archery—an important skill in time of war against the French.

60 Hornchurch's secluded railway station about 1913. Neat curtains at all the windows of the stationmaster's house prevent passengers from looking in although somebody is looking out at the foursome waiting by the road. When Hornchurch finally got its railway—rather late in the day in 1885—what had already been described in 1876 as a rather 'large and busy-looking industrial village was going to spread eventually across the fields and farms and become a large Urban District.

61 A Southend train hurtles through the Hornchurch platforms of the London Tilbury and Southend Railway, *c*.1910. The wholesale development of the district did not immediately follow the construction of the line, bringing the village within half an hour's distance from London. It was 10 years before William Carter of Parkstone, Dorset, purchased the southern part of the Manor of Nelmes of 200 acres plus some other land to start developing the Emerson Park Estate.

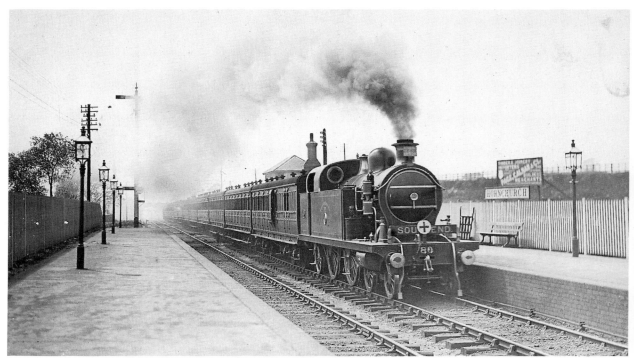

62 The *Railway Hotel*, seen here about 1911, only followed the station after a number of years on what had been open fields, farming land and a sports field.

63 Nelmes Manor House in the 1950s. Although the southern portion of its estate was sold off for development, Nelmes remained in fairly secluded surroundings as did many other old buildings in Hornchurch. It was a beautiful old mansion which had been altered during the reign of Elizabeth I by the Roche family. Sir William Roche, Lord Mayor of London in 1540, was one of the owners. The 20th century has taken its toll and Nelmes Manor was bulldozed in 1967, the day before the Civic Amenities Act came into force, as the owner felt he could not afford to restore it—a sad end to an ancient home.

Industries and the First World War

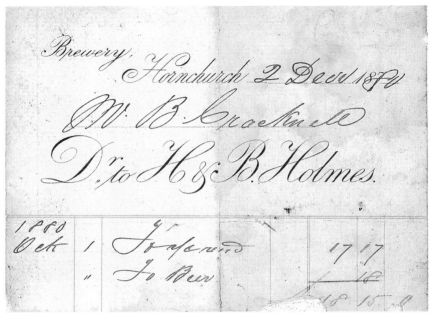

64a Billhead for the Hornchurch Brewery, 1880. The Holmes Brothers owned the Brewery from 1874-1892. From 1892 to its demise in 1925 it was owned by the Conron family.

64b A plan of Hornchurch Brewery at the beginning of the 20th century. The business was founded in 1789 by John Woodfine, and his family were involved up to 1874. The buildings nearer to the *White Hart* were erected around 1838 by Thomas Woodfine and, as shown on the plan, a lot of buildings were squeezed into quite a small area. An interesting account of the Brewery is published in the *Havering History Review* Nos. 5 and 6.

CHURCH STREET, HORNCHURCH

65 In this 1914 photograph the Brewery Office on the left is in deep shadow, as was often the case, but the houses opposite are in bright sunlight. This is the Hornchurch all the soldiers came to know including the *King's Head* opposite which was, of course, one of the fifty or so public houses supplied with Old Hornchurch Brewery's beer. However the New Zealand Military Hospital at Grey Towers was serviced by Ind Coope and had subsidised beer, making it the cheapest pint in town.

66 These two Bell-ringers' pitchers, now kept in the church, were connected with two Hornchurch industries. The smaller is of brownish earthenware with a dull glaze, and is inscribed '1731, Hornchurch Essex' with the names of ringers and churchwardens of the time. The larger is of very dark appearance with a thick glaze that looks almost purple in colour—this is inscribed 24 May 1815. This pitcher made by Rt. Aungier with the names of churchwardens and ringers of that date—on it is the wording 'Gift of Mr. C. Cove'. It seems likely that both were manufactured at Cove's Pottery which had been formerly established at the corner of Abbs Cross Lane and High Street since the early 17th century. Ale brewed at Hornchurch Hall was on occasion supplied to the ringers in these pitchers but they were at one stage kept at the *King's Head* and filled with Hornchurch Brewery ale.

67a In the 1920s the entrance to Wedlake's Fairkytes Foundry is tucked away on the right of this photograph of Billet Lane, almost overwhelmed with trees. The site is now a green open space below the Queen's Theatre. Thomas the businessman and Robert the engineer came to Hornchurch in 1784 to found a firm whose agricultural implements became famous all over Britain. Robert Wedlake invented among other implements a double-action haymaking machine which continued to be used for over a century.

    67b Looking through the gates of the Foundry from a prospectus issued by Mary Wedlake, widow of Thomas, who continued to run the firm from the 1820s onward.

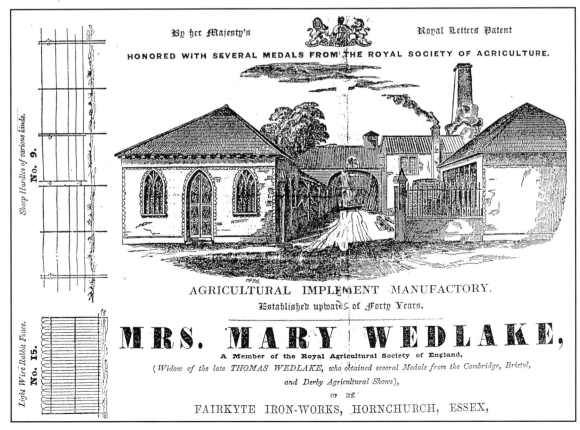

By her Majesty's   Royal Letters Patent

HONORED WITH SEVERAL MEDALS FROM THE ROYAL SOCIETY OF AGRICULTURE.

Sheep Hurdles of various kinds. **No. 9.**

Light Wire Rabbit Fence. **No. 15.**

AGRICULTURAL IMPLEMENT MANUFACTORY.

Established upwards of Forty Years.

MRS. MARY WEDLAKE,

A Member of the Royal Agricultural Society of England,

(*Widow of the late THOMAS WEDLAKE, who obtained several Medals from the Cambridge, Bristol, and Derby Agricultural Shows*),

OF THE

FAIRKYTE IRON-WORKS, HORNCHURCH, ESSEX,

"FAIR KYTES" HORNCHURCH.

860.

68 Opposite Fairkytes Foundry was Fairkytes house itself—the style of the iron gateposts and railings suggests that they were made at the foundry. The present house, which still stands, dates from the mid-18th century but the records show a house of this name here in 1520. Thomas Wedlake is supposed to have lived here from his arrival in Hornchurch and it was later occupied by Joseph Fry, son of Elizabeth the prison reformer.

69 An important local trader in the early 20th century was F.W. Aley, baker and confectioner, whose shop in the High Street was pictured in that section. This scene is about 1908.

70 In north-west Hornchurch the site later occupied by the Roneo Works was at first a cycle factory whose name is commemorated in a housing development in what is now South Street, Ormonde Court. In 1890 it was listed as the St Andrew's Cycle Works but later became the New Ormonde Cycle factory and was one of the ventures of a well-known millionaire promoter of the 1890s—Terence Hooley. He had promoted Bovril, Dunlop tyres and above all the cult of the bicycle, which was an incredible craze at the turn of the century, involving every household.

71 These Roneo employees assembled outside the works in 1912 marked five years of the new firm's progress at Haveringwell as this hamlet was known. Terence Hooley's playboy style of living which even infiltrated a current music-hall song—'Terah-rah-Hooley-ay...'—came to an end in bankruptcy. Before this happened he closed the cycle works which was used for a while by the Ramie Fibre Co., who made gas mantles for both home and street lighting. In the 1902 *Directory* an entry appears for the Ormonde Spinning Syndicate Ltd., fibre spinners, so the name had stuck. There now came into the picture A.D. Klaber who had acquired the rights to rotary duplicators, imported and put together in this country. Needing greater capacity Klaber discovered the old Ormonde premises in 1906 and by May 1907 the factory had taken over the site, moving from its previous premises at Great Eastern Street in London.

72 Roneo Factory, the Engineering Section Assembly line—after manufacturing munitions in the First World War plus office equipment for the forces, the factory geared up for peacetime production and expansion again.

73 Roneo Factory and neighbourhood in 1930 from the air. The Hornchurch Road encircles the Hornchurch Urban District land which includes all the works and the gravel pits, beyond where Lyon Road industrial estate now lies. On the north-west side of the road (now called South Street) is the Romford Water Works and Office.

ROMFORD SOUVENIR OF THE HERO WHO BROUGHT DOWN ZEP. "L.21" AT CUFFLEY ON SEP. 3RD 1916.

High Street.

LIEU. WILLIAM LEEFE ROBINSON, V.C.

Market Place.

74 William Leefe Robinson, VC, the Conquering Hero, September 1916. Idolised like a pop star as sportsmen and actors had been before him, Robinson, whose feat of Zeppelin-bashing is described on the card, was one of 'the few' of the First World War conflict who were based at another old Hornchurch estate—at Suttons Aerodrome which had been part of Tom Crawford's Suttons Farm. Here Romford is anxious to claim a share of his fame by issuing a souvenir card. Nationally the production of such mementoes amounted to a sizeable industry and Hornchurch's own photographers like Frank Luff and Bursall Tonge fought for their share of the glory of what was at first known as the Royal Flying Corps but matured at the end of the war into the Royal Air Force.

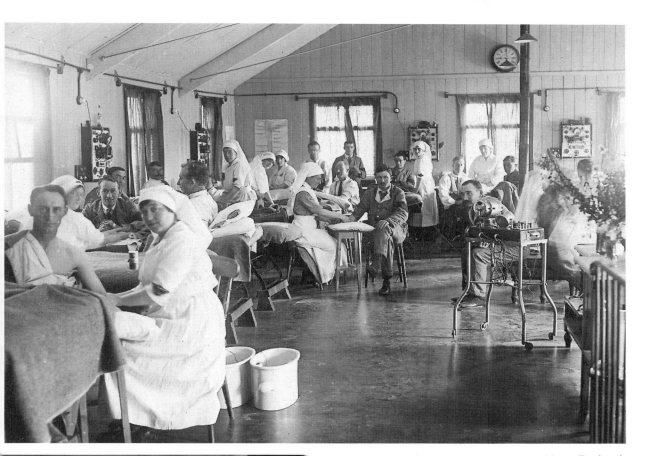

75 A corner of the massage room—New Zealand Convalescent Hospital, Grey Towers. After the Sportsmen departed for France, Grey Towers Camp became a home for the Royal Army Service Corps (their brief stay is commemorated in 'Pioneer House', North Street) and then the base camp and later convalescent hospital for their New Zealand soldiers who fought in the First World War. They have left their mark, sadly, in some graves in Hornchurch Cemetery and, more joyfully, with the many English girls from Hornchurch who married New Zealanders and went to live in New Zealand. The nurses and sisters in this picture are, however, from New Zealand.

76 New Zealand wounded at work on therapeutic handicrafts. Like the Americans in a later conflict, no expense was spared by the New Zealand government and people to make the lives of their soldiers as comfortable as possible at least at base camps. Some of these men endured terrible hardship and stress in the Gallipoli campaign and, of course, conditions in France were also vile. The story of Gallipoli as experienced by the New Zealanders is told in a book by Barbara Mannox—*Hornchurch and the New Zealand Connection*.

77 New Zealand 'blue boys' crafting picture frames and Art Nouveau metalwork. Grey Towers was fully equipped for all these activities and in addition further accommodation was available for recuperating soldiers at outstations such as 'Te Whare Puni' (The Meeting House) in Butts Green Road which is illustrated in *Bygone Hornchurch and Upminster*.

78 We leave the New Zealanders recuperating in the sun on a Hornchurch farm, haymaking in 1917. Those that survived lived to remember their Hornchurch days with fondness, others struggled to overcome damage to limbs and loss of function.

ALFRED HARVEY,

Auctioneer, Valuer, Estate Agent,

AND PUBLIC HOUSE BROKER,

HAVERING-WELL HOUSE, ROMFORD.

Houses, Land, Farming Stock, Furniture, and every description of Property Sold.

INVENTORIES & VALUATIONS MADE FOR ADMINISTRATION & OTHER PURPOSES.

SEVERAL PUBLIC HOUSES, BEER HOUSES, BUSINESS HOUSES, AND PRIVATE HOUSES TO LET.

LEASEHOLD AND FREEHOLD HOUSES AND VILLAS FOR SALE.

PLOTS OF FREEHOLD BUILDING LAND FOR SALE.

No charge made if business is not effected, and for Sales by Auction the charges are strictly moderate. Prompt settlements. Security given to any amount if required.

Agent to the Royal Farmers Life and Fire Insurance Company.

Any person seeking a Business of any description, wishing to purchase Freehold or Leasehold Property, or having any Business or Property to dispose of, should apply at once.

Offices:—56, Bishopgate Within, London; Stratford "Express" Office, Stratford, Essex; Opposite the Corn Exchange, Romford.

---

79 This early house and estate agent's advertisement appeared in 1872. Nearly all the business was with farmers, public houses and business premises. However, two lines remind us of the beginning of a residential boom, however small and slow-moving—Private Houses TO LET—Leasehold and Freehold Houses and Villas For Sale. Havering Well House was on the Park Lane end of the site on which Roneo's factory developed.

80 Lower Brentwood Road (the Hornchurch side) about the turn of the century. Park Lane starts where the delivery cart on the right is standing by the gaslamp. This area's Victorian development owes much to its position near Romford. Continuous streets were not a feature of Hornchurch at this time, and Brentwood Road did not have continuous numbering of houses until well into this century. Instead it was broken into small groupings such as Ongar Villas, Malvern Villas, Stanley Villas and Bedford Cottages, showing how the housing was gradually erected by small builders who would then sell them or, more likely, let them on a weekly basis. There were also some individual properties such as Daydawn and Glendale, built on a more generous scale. C.J. Skinner, whose shop is behind the smart carriage, probably lived above the shop at Park Villas. The man in the trap may be Mr. Mason, the shopkeeper.

81 Holy Cross Church, temporary building, corner of Malvern Road/Park Lane, 1920. New churches in the form of temporary buildings were often provided for growing residential areas although they often lived on as a church hall after a permanent church was built. This particular hut had been transferred from use as a chapel in the army camp at Grey Towers.

82 Further new buildings are going up next to Hornchurch bus garage in this mid-1930s view. Many shops opened to serve the new roads behind the Hornchurch Road.

83 The post office, hardware and leather shop mean business with their hard-to-miss 'brutalist' lettering and no-nonsense air. The year is 1931 in Hornchurch Road.

84 The Council Cottages in Abbs Cross Lane with delivery-man from the Old Hornchurch Brewery. After the First World War local councils were empowered to construct council dwellings, if they so wished, the Government providing subsidies. Romford Rural District Council built houses in several suitable locations. These particular dwellings were actually built in 1913, before this legislation was thought of, by R.R.D.C. at the prompting of Hornchurch Parish, who were thus ahead of the trend.

85 By 1923 Abbs Cross Lane had acquired a cross-section of housing types as this picture shows. There were Victorian farm labourers' cottages as well as some ribbon development, and some larger private houses, both for sale and to rent.

86 Curtis Road ends in grassland as development temporarily comes to a halt in the 1920s. Much of Hornchurch and Upminster was developed as rows of bungalows or chalet bungalows, so this type of scene is very familiar locally. However, the surrounding Emerson Park Estate, from its origin in 1895, consisted chiefly of substantial family homes in large grounds. Curtis Road now continues through the former grassed area and today looks quite different, the houses being shaded by mature trees and bushes. It was named after the site manager of the estate, Mr. W.H. Curtis.

87 A Hornchurch housebuilder's advertisement, April 1934. These houses were very conveniently placed with the new Upminster Bridge station (on the District Line) close at hand and an excellent bus service along the Hornchurch Road.

88 Several items are being delivered to homes to Cecil Avenue about 1936. Two houses are offered for sale by R.C. Ridgwell and the Parkside Estate Office, Ardleigh Green. Perhaps the owners are in trouble with the mortgage company, in which case they will find plenty of properties to rent, or perhaps the neighbourhood is too quiet, a common problem for those who had grown up in the city.

89 Scenes at Ardleigh Green Junior Mixed and Infants School, Ardleigh Green Road, opened as a council school in 1933-4 to cater for a growing population in this district.

90 Woodhall Parade, a good example of a small shopping parade in a mainly residential district of the 1930s.

91 A post-war Hornchurch Urban District Council Meeting with a full attendance of councillors (known as members), committee clerks, officers and pressmen. The council chamber with its bull's head emblem still exists at the time of

writing although it is no longer used for council meetings. Langtons House was given to Hornchurch Council in 1929 three years after its formation. The new local government area started from scratch without records or any item of equipment, but gradually established itself to fulfil the many important functions necessary in such a rapidly growing district. It became a very competent council and made wise decisions in many areas, such as the creation of urban footpaths and parks and the management of environmental health. Hornchurch, after some areas had been added, was eventually the largest council in England measured by land area.

The Earliest Road
Upminster from West to East

The long evolution of mankind in Upminster has gradually been revealed over the last century or so. Each era has left some legacy of its existence. In 1890 a member of the Essex Field Club, on his way to a club meeting in Upminster, discovered a Paleolithic or early Stone-Age flint implement in the fields north of Tylers Common. Traces of late Bronze-Age man (1000-700 B.C.) have been discovered in recent years at Hunts Hill Farm. Also on this site, excavation has revealed occupation during the Iron Ages. Early Iron-Age pottery, thought to date from the 5th or 4th century B.C., has surfaced. A two-handed bowl of this period may be a copy of a metal vessel. Travelling forward in time, a small enclosure at Hunts Hill may date from the Early or Middle Iron Age. The extensive Middle Iron-Age settlement here included at least five round houses of varying dates. In the late Iron Age a settlement on the site was defended by a rectangular enclosure, with ditches two metres in depth, accompanied by an earth rampart backed by a timber revetment dominating the hilltop. An amphora or Roman wine jar was discovered at this settlement in 1995, indicating that these people had made contact with the Romans.

The Roman period in Upminster, as in surrounding areas like Rainham, is characterised by scattered farming centres. At Hunts Hill evidence of this activity comes from the finding of a small cut-up plough, the remains of which lay beneath one of several Roman wells. Constructed on top was a well-made timber framework housing the well. Large quantities of Roman pottery of the 2nd and 3rd centuries were discovered in ditches near the main Roman living area. A rather makeshift late Roman well, found a few years before, contained many dung beetles; a sure sign that there had been grazing animals. In addition the preserved head of a honey bee suggested Roman apiaries for honey production. A kiln-like structure was also investigated. In the 1960s some ditched enclosures at another site at Bush Farm, Corbets Tey were excavated. This site was revealed as a first-century Romano-British farmstead. Three of the pottery items found are illustrated in the final section of this book. The settlement consisted of simple huts occupied throughout the first century A.D. and also later during the third century.

Prelude to the Middle Ages

In adjoining fields at Hunts Hill Farm the Passmore Edwards (Newham) Museum Service excavated the remains of a small Saxon settlement and an early Saxon cemetery with graves of varying sizes, probably to accommodate family groups. Most of the dead had a small iron knife placed beside them at burial; one was buried with a small, grass-tempered pot and a knife. Some of these South Essex Saxon communities are now believed to have been recruited by the last Romans to help fight off the attacks of further intruders to the east coast. The Saxons and the Romano-Britons may have inter-bred to a certain extent and become the later Saxons. What is known is that Tertullian speaks of parts of Britain that were inaccessible to the Romans but which had been 'conquered by Christ'. This was as early as A.D. 208. Christianity certainly grew during the third and fourth centuries in parts of Britain, three bishops—Eborius of York, Restitutus of London and Adelphius of Caerleon—attended the Council of Arles in A.D. 314. However there were many who worshipped other gods and leaders such as our putative local hero 'Horn'. Early in the fifth century, the Romans abandoned England and invading armies of heathen Saxons, Jutes and Angles swarmed in from the east coast overwhelming the Christian church—the faith surviving only in the west. Pope Gregory, elected in 590, selected a monk from his own priory, Augustine, to lead a missionary band to England and he, remarkably, succeeded in converting the King of Kent and his court soon after he arrived in 597. To the north of Kent, Pagan kingdoms prevented further conversion. In 653 King Penda of Mercia, a Pagan who had previously banned Christians from his sphere of influence, relented and allowed priests into his territory, one of whom was St Cedd who quite soon came south from the midlands and entered Essex. Having been made a bishop he set up missions at Tilbury and Bradwell and quite possibly at Upminster as well. Upminster church at first served a wide area and a predecessor of the original *Bell Inn* on the corner opposite may have been set up originally as a kind of church hostel. At the south end of Upminster parish is the place known as Chafford Heath, named after Bishop Chad, the second Bishop of London. After the Conquest the village church and inn would provide temporary resting places for thousands of pilgrims travelling from the north of the district, making eventually for the shrine of St Thomas à Becket at Canterbury.

92 Hornchurch Road, running down to the railway bridge and the old road bridge boundary over the river between Hornchurch and Upminster, 1908. If we are right, this is the oldest element in the history of the two parishes. The ancient leader Horn trod this way with his followers—it bisected his territory. The sylvan charm of this stretch leading to the ancient village of Upminster strips away the centuries.

93 We are now approaching the bridge and what was once also a ford. Upminster Hill beyond the Bridge House is besieged by trees—this is 1912. In the past, farmers in the fields this side of the bridge are said to have found hundreds of human bones. Was this the site of an ancient battle between two groups disputing territory?

94 Halfway up Upminster Hill the landscape begins to open out, 1908. There are some interesting weather-boarded houses on the south side of the road (demolished 1909). Out of sight on the right-hand side are the ancient cottages which used to form Upminster Workhouse before Oldchurch in Romford became the Poor House for the whole area. They were converted back into ordinary homes by George Rowe after 1836. On the left the bottom end of Minster House School is in view—it had been a school from before the 19th century.

95 At the top of the hill in the 1920s. The old chapel on the left was built in 1801. It was the Congregational place of worship until the new church opened in Station Road (1911). Although showing its age, it is amazing to think that both this building and the windmill opposite, built in 1803, are still with us. There is a link in that James Nokes the builder of the mill was a prominent member of the chapel's congregation.

96 Opposite the old chapel was the Manse, the minister's house. This was a solid building of 1873, taken down in the mid-1930s, and seen on the right. Opposite, above the chapel, an outbuilding projects where there once was an 18th-century boys' private school and now the buildings behind Hill Place have become a Catholic girls' school.

97 Upminster Mill, *c.*1900. Built by James Nokes to supply a demand for milling capacity during the Napoleonic Wars, it was once supplied with wheat from the surrounding fields which Nokes had also purchased. Later a steam auxiliary mill was added. In this century home-milled wheat began to lose ground to that imported by ship from the North American prairies. The mill resorted to grinding patent cattle food in its latter years and finally closed in 1934. For most of its 131 years of working life the mill was passed down through the Abraham family. The mill, after its closure, was almost demolished and its land given over to houses. However, local people intervened and it is now owned by the local council, and opened on certain summer weekends by Hornchurch Historical Society members.

98 The approach to the Bell crossroads before any development had taken place. This is the area once occupied by the village green. Sir James Esdaile after 1770 took down the old *Bell Inn*, which lay far back, and rebuilt it here. Other parts of the green lay under the part of the churchyard on the right of this scene (it had previously been the rector's garden). The house on the left, Mr. Aggiss's 'Chestnuts', and its garden occupied another part and the wide pavement which can still be seen on the east side of Station Road corner was the final part of the green.

99 The first roundabout, with road signs, at the Bell corner. The house and shop known as 'Cosy Corner' is open for business on the right. Now demolished, there is only the spacious piece of pavement to remind us of the lost corner of village green on which it was built. The beginning of Station Road is behind the parked council trailer.

St. Mary's Library.

100 This is the quiet rural scene along St Mary's Lane that greeted the traveller in 1899. Until 1922 this road was known as Cranham Lane. The gentleman with the walking stick often appears in photographs of this time—he is T.L. Wilson who wrote the *History and Topography of Upminster* in 1880-1. He is almost certainly standing next to his own fence—his builder's yard was in the garden. For 30 years he was in partnership with Edward Hook in numerous building works and they jointly owned the brickworks in Bird Lane. He also sometimes acted as an estate agent, receiving £80 commission when the *Bell Inn* was sold to Mr. F. Seabrook in 1886.

101 Oak Place, a charming Georgian house, was built about 1740 and lived in by the Rev. J. Jubb, curate of St Lawrence's Church from 1737-63. The building has a magnificent cellar divided into two by a 2-ft.-thick curved brick arch. It is by the bend in the road and by the 1930s was converted into two shops—the cinema being built opposite. This photograph of *c.*1907 shows a cart in the middle of the road, loaded with baskets of agricultural produce.

102 The Clock House along St Mary's Lane, seen here in the 1950s, was the stable block to New Place which is the building shown in *Bygone Hornchurch and Upminster* (plate 50). New Place Estate occupied the whole of the south side of St Mary's Lane from the *Bell Inn* to the Argyle Gardens of today and back as far as Sunnyside Gardens. The last version of the house, built by Sir James Esdaile in 1775, lay further back from St Mary's Lane, nearer the *Bell,* and had a large, many mirrored drawing room which was used for balls, as Sir James was very fond of dancing. The turret clock on the Clock House was of interesting design and its chimes kept the whole village on time in the days when there were few other timepieces.

103 Further along the lane, in 1910, were these old weather-boarded buildings with the *Mason's Arms* beyond. A new inn building was erected in 1928, the one shown here having been licensed since the 19th century.

104 Nearing Cranham, these rural cottages are well looked after with typical cottage-garden flowers and plants at the front. Most of the cottages were badly damaged in the Second World War and some were subsequently demolished.

Cranham Road.

105 Down a long chase of the Cranham Road stood All Saints' Church. This drawing shows it in 1872 before it was demolished, being in a bad state of dilapidation. It had been built in the 13th century possessing nave, chancel, south porch and low weather-boarded west tower. It was replaced by the present structure, built 1873-5 and designed by Richard Armstrong. Most of the £5,114 in cost to build was donated by Richard Benyon, owner of Cranham Hall, next door.

106 Cranham Hall, *c.*1916. In the 18th century there came to the predecessor of this house a very famous man of the time—General James Oglethorpe. Two of his diverse achievements were the Foundation of the State of Georgia, U.S.A. and the creation of the British Herring Industry. The house of that time was a brick mansion, built about 1600, and set near the north-east corner of a walled garden of about one and a half acres. There was also a small park to the south and east.

107a (*top left*) Impression of James Oglethorpe based on a mezzotint of about 1744. One of the causes which Oglethorpe took up as an M.P. was that against the indignities of imprisonment for debt. His plan was to found a colony to which 'poor and honest industrious debtors' could be sent.

107b (*above*) General Oglethorpe's statue in Savannah, Georgia. Georgia became the 13th and last of Britain's American colonies and the one which had a great struggle to survive. But Oglethorpe never wavered in his determination to make the colony viable though it was underfinanced by the trustees in London. He personally took an idealistic gamble, financing the colony's defence out of his own pocket for five years, but Georgia finally became a success and Oglethorpe achieved his aims.

107c (*left*) Oglethorpe is thought to have been the author of this optimistic pamphlet that brought support for the Georgia scheme from the British public and lured great numbers of potential colonists.

108 (*right*) Lady Wright of Cranham Hall became Lady Elizabeth Oglethorpe. After the vicissitudes of his public life, which had brought him almost to the brink of ruin, James Oglethorpe finally escaped his enemies, who sought to have him court-martialled, and spent much of his later life at Cranham Hall, having married its heiress. Here he was visited by the famous of the day such as Samuel Johnson, James Boswell, Oliver Goldsmith and Sir Joshua Reynolds, whose portrait of Oglethorpe was unfortunately destroyed by fire.

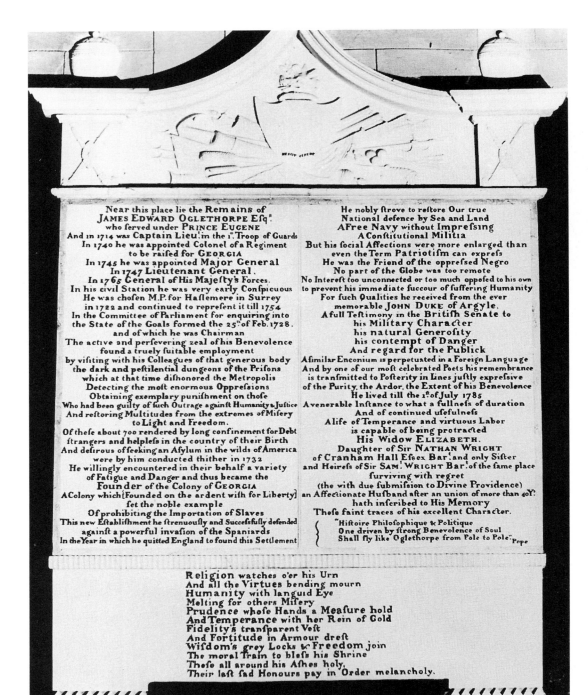

Near this place lie the Remains of
JAMES EDWARD OGLETHORPE Esq:
who served under PRINCE EUGENE
And in 1714 was Captain Lieu: in the 1:t Troop of Guards
In 1740 he was appointed Colonel of a Regiment
to be raised for GEORGIA
In 1745 he was appointed Major General
In 1747 Lieutenant General.
In 1765 General of His Majesty's Forces.
In his civil Station he was very early Conspicuous
He was chosen M.P. for Haslemere in Surrey
in 1722 and continued to represent it till 1754
In the Committee of Parliament for enquiring into
the State of the Goals formed the 25:th of Feb. 1728.
and of which he was Chairman
The active and persevering zeal of his Benevolence
found a truely suitable employment
by visiting with his Colleagues of that generous body
the dark and pestilential dungeons of the Prisons
which at that time dishonored the Metropolis
Detecting the most enormous Oppresions
Obtaining exemplary punishment on those
Who had been guilty of such Outrage against Humanity & Justice
And restoring Multitudes from the extremes of Misery
to Light and Freedom.
Of these about 700 rendered by long confinement for Debt
strangers and helpless in the country of their Birth
And desirous of seeking an Asylum in the wilds of America
were by him conducted thither in 1732
He willingly encountered in their behalf a variety
of Fatigue and Danger and thus became the
Founder of the Colony of GEORGIA
A Colony which [Founded on the ardent wish for Liberty]
set the noble example
Of prohibiting the Importation of Slaves
This new Establishment he strenuously and Succesfully defended
against a powerful invasion of the Spaniards
In the Year in which he quitted England to found this Settlement

He nobly strove to restore Our true
National defence by Sea and Land
A Free Navy without Impressing
A Constitutional Militia
But his social Affections were more enlarged than
even the Term Patriotism can express
He was the Friend of the oppresed Negro
No part of the Globe was too remote
No Interest too unconnected or too much oppos'd to his own
to prevent his immediate succour of suffering Humanity
For such Qualities he received from the ever
memorable JOHN DUKE of Argyle.
A full Testimony in the British Senate to
his Military Character
his natural Generosity
his contempt of Danger
And regard for the Publick
A similar Enconium is perpetuated in a Foreign Language
And by one of our most celebrated Poets his remembrance
is transmitted to Posterity in Lines justly expressive
of the Purity, the Ardor, the Extent of his Benevolence
He lived till the 1:st of July 1785
A venerable Instance to what a fullness of duration
And of continued usefulness
A life of Temperance and virtuous Labor
is capable of being protracted
His Widow ELIZABETH,
Daughter of Sir NATHAN WRIGHT
of Cranham Hall Essex Bar: and only Sister
and Heiress of Sir SAM: WRIGHT Bar: of the same place
surviving with regret
(the with due submission to Divine Providence)
an Affectionate Husband after an union of more than 40Y:
hath inscribed to His Memory
These faint traces of his excellent Character.

{ "Histoire Philosophique & Politique
One driven by strong Benevolence of Soul
Shall fly like Oglethorpe from Pole to Pole." Pope

Religion watches o'er his Urn
And all the Virtues bending mourn
Humanity with languid Eye
Melting for others Misery
Prudence whose Hands a Measure hold
And Temperance with her Rein of Gold
Fidelity's transparent Vest
And Fortitude in Armour drest
Wisdom's grey Locks & Freedom join
The moral Train to bless his Shrine
These all around his Ashes holy,
Their last sad Honours pay in Order melancholy.

His disconsolate Widow died the 26th of Oct: 1787. in
her 79th Year, and is buried with him in the vault
in the center of this Chancel.
Her Fortitude of mind and extensive Charity deserve
to be remembered, tho' her own Modesty would desire
them to be forgot,

109 Oglethorpe's splendid marble monument recording his achievements and virtues was rescued from the old church of All Saints and placed on the south chancel wall of the new. It is one of the places of pilgrimage for Americans from the state he nurtured into life. Nowhere else perhaps in so small a church does such a large monument make an attempt to chronicle all the achievements of a lifetime's battle against 'conventional' thinking.

110 Talking shop for the village of Cranham—the post office in the 1930s.

111 East of Cranham is the old 15th-century manor house known as Franks.

112 Looking from the bottom of Station Road, *c*.1911. Shopping parades already line the eastern side of the road, but the other side on the left of this view is still relatively undeveloped.

113 Further along Station Road we get a better view of the traders in about 1911. Searson Brothers, the long established shoe shop, is one above the nearest white painted frontage which is Thompson and Rice, fishmongers. Below them is Harry Talbot the greengrocer. Nearest the camera the aproned man is standing outside A.E. Wooff's Dining Rooms.

UPMINSTER CONGREGATIONAL CHURCH, FROM ST LAWRENCE RD.

114 Looking west across Station Road to Gaynes Road, *c.*1914. Note the vacant plot on the left at the bottom of the road.

115 St Lawrence Road, facing east, 1912.

116 A maid in uniform *de rigeur* has been sent out to purchase muffins or some teatime delicacy for her mistress at Upminster's first shopping parade next to the station. Opened in 1907, it is still giving service; a pub called the *Essex Yeoman* was built on the north end where the rather strange garden supplies plot was situated.

117 The staff and produce of Tollworthy's butchers are on display in this splendid photograph of an individual shop in the parade, 1928.

118 The outstanding delivery fleet belonging to Tollworthy's, 1928. Many Upminster housewives by this time were telephoning the shop for their supplies—no need to send the maid out any more.

119 A little later, motor cars have taken over in front of the parade.

120 Going back in time, horsecabs look for custom as passengers leave the old entrance of Upminster station about 1912—most of this building still remains.

St. Marys
Library

121   A Grays to Romford train waits for the all clear signal at the mainline platform about 1914.

122 Upminster station in the 1920s—a Romford train on the middle platform.

123 Upminster in L.M.S. days, June 1938. This scene has a touch of the Rev. Awdry's books about it; one almost expects to see the approach of the Fat Controller. The engine and carriages are neat and tidy and there is not a scrap of litter to be seen.

124 Hall Lane, looking towards the station bridge, 1911.

125 Upminster Court, a masterpiece of high Edwardian design in 1916. The architect was Charles Reilly who lived at High House near Upminster Church. It was built in 1905/6 for A.E. Williams, a director of Samuel Williams Ltd. This picture was taken looking towards the stable block, shortly after construction. Each part of Upminster Court has its own delightful features. The garden frontage overlooking the Ingrebourne Valley is particularly fine.

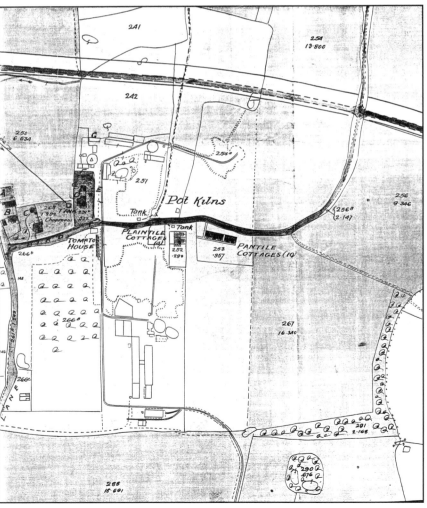

126 Pantile cottages, Bird Lane, were associated with the brick, tile and drainpipe works in this lane which operated for nearly 150 years. The brick kiln, which was at the entrance to Bird Lane from Hall Lane and opposite Chapman's Farm, was built by Matthew Howland Patrick in 1774. He married the widow of Champion Branfill II (1712-60). Specimens of the products of these works are preserved in the Upminster Tithe Barn Museum. E.J. Brown, the latterday owner, laid down a track to connect with the main railway line, portions of which were still to be seen in the 1960s.

127 Plan of the Pot Kilns area. Notice the railway track running through the works.

South to Corbets Tey

128 Post Office Cottages, Corbets Tey Road—there is quite a turnout of adults and children to see the photographer at work and also to have their picture taken. The male figure standing behind the line of boys appears to be T.L. Wilson, Upminster's historian, getting in the frame again. Woolworths and Macdonalds now trade in the parade of shops which replaced these cottages.

129 Looking south in 1910 from the top end of Corbets Tey Road towards the location in the last picture, with the local policeman, probably P.C. Beasley, keeping a wary eye. Upminster got its first county copper, J. Webb, in 1886. He was followed in 1896 by others, most notably in 1901 by Constable Beasley who had an incredible knack of being in the right place at the right time. In September 1910 he stopped a runaway horse, whilst in February 1911 he was quickly on the spot and taking charge when a stray bull found its way into Henry Talbot's Station Road greengrocer's shop. Also in 1910, finding lambs dead in a field, he watched out for and spied two dogs worrying sheep. Beating them off, he followed them home. In December of that year Beasley found the dead body of a local man on Upminster Hall Farm. This turned out to be birdscarer Robert Shelley—possibly living rough and unwell, he had been advised to go to the workhouse and infirmary, but death struck before he got there. An entertaining account of crime and the police in Upminster can be found in the W.E.A. *Story of Upminster*, Book 11.

130 Looking north to the shopping part of Corbets Tey Road, *c.*1933. Behind the conifer tree, hedge and fence on the left stands Hoppy Hall, a late 16th/early 17th-century house, pulled down in 1935/6 and now a car park. It was latterly the home of the family of Wedgwood Benn. South of this point Corbets Tey Road, once skirted by the parkland of Gaynes and farmland, has now become solidly residential.

131 Foxhall was an unusual building with an original centre portion with steps up to an ornamental front door built in 1718. It was at one time called Vauxhall or Foxhunters Hall, which may have been too elaborate for the locals. Wings were added to the north-west and south-west corners in 1817 and there were 14 acres of land attached. The house was sold in 1923 and demolished shortly afterwards, the land being divided and developed for housing.

132 Corbets Tey Village, *c.*1922. The post office waits quietly in the sun for customers. On the right the corner house with a hedge round the window is the former *George Inn*, once the *Royal George* and in 1835 the *George and Dragon*. The inn was closed on 10 October 1901—the landlord, Thomas Starr, sold the last glass of beer to William Snell, a local shoemaker—since when the property has been a private house. The *Huntsmen and Hounds* dating from the 18th century but was rebuilt, reopening on 28 May 1896 as the *Huntsman* (singular) *and Hounds*— a subtle alteration.

133 The garden front of High House, Corbets Tey village, *c.*1916. This unusual building, usually pictured from the front, has a narrow and elegant late 17th-century brick façade built beside a lower, earlier timber-framed wing on the east side. A spacious staircase with a curved rail speaks of occupation by men of taste. It was inhabited by Thomas Mayor until 1768 and, after this, held by Thomas London, the parish doctor who later went to 'Londons' Corbets Tey Road. In 1804 it was taken over as a school by John Saunders, exempt from service in the Napoleonic Wars because of lameness in one arm. Nearly thirty years later Saunders went bankrupt and, when the house was put up for auction, it was given this delightful description '... large garden and 30 acres ... 20 bedsteads, 20 feather beds, 30 pairs of blankets, quilts and counterpanes, curtains, carpets, bedlinen, plate, books, gloves, cooking and washing utensils, stoves, patent kitchen range, desks, haystack, wheatstack, bay mare, cart etc.'.

134 The quaint Tey Stores and the Octagon, 1960.

135 (*right*) The more interesting south front of Stubbers in 1920, a mansion with a long history, taking its name from William Stubber, the yeoman who created it between 1439 and his death in 1484. The history of the units of land which he brought together can be traced back even earlier to documents of 1334. The house of the 16th century grew and altered over a period of 300 years and with successive owners. A particularly interesting owner was William Coys, a famous botanist who grew many plants at Stubbers for the first time in this country including the Jerusalem artichoke. He also introduced the use of hops combined with barley, for the making of English beer. Previously a concoction of malt and water known as wort served the purpose of English drinkers. Coys' garden at Stubbers was the Kew Gardens of its time and he exchanged plants with many other botanists.

136 (*left*) William Russell (1633-1705) made his fortune from a draper's shop in the City of London which flourished with the return to the throne of Charles II and the consequent revival of interest in fine clothes. Russell eventually became alderman and sheriff of the City. In 1679 the king made Russell a knight, an honour which some believe was compensation for money which Charles II owed him—this often being the way with the king's debts. In 1689 Sir William marked his status by purchasing Stubbers. It was to remain in the Russell family's hands for 300 years.

137 (*left*) The Pigeon House at Stubbers, built in 1797, was a surprising building. Although many dovehouses existed in the grounds of large houses they were not always as impressive as this one. The construction was of timber, lath and plaster on top of a brick base eight feet high. Human access was by means of a long ladder. In the upper storey were 662 wood and clay nesting boxes.

138 The scattered village of North Ockendon has two nuclei: one is the church and the other is around the *White Horse*, seen here in about 1900.

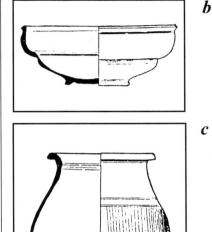

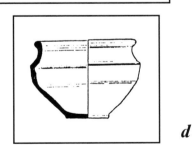

a *(above)* A Roman flagon (soft orange paste with cream slip).

b *(top right)* Cup of grey paste and polished black surface (Dragendorf catalogue form 27) similar to items from Richborough, Kent. Like Rainham further south a considerable amount of material has gradually surfaced during gravel digging showing occupation of the area during most of the periods of evolution of early man.

c *(right)* Butt beaker made from sandy, grey paste similar to items known in Camulodunum (Colchester).

d *(bottom right)* A wide-mouthed Roman bowl with formed neck and dark burnished finish.

139 Earthenware found in a ditched enclosure at Corbets Tey, identified as a Romano-British farmstead of simple huts, occupied throughout the first century and also during the third century A.D.

UPMINSTER RECTORY AND CHURCH . 10

PUBLISHED BY
D. A. RAMSAY

140 (*above*) St Laurence's Church tower and rectory. The western end of the Church has stood since the late 12th/early 13th centuries. The Rev. Samuel Bradshaw (1735-69) built the present rectory.

(*left*) Title page of Derham's *The Artificial Clockmaker*, the first book on practical clock and watchmaking written in English.

(*below*) The most famous rector was William Derham, who combined his work in the church with scientific research, corresponding with many other men of science of his day (1689-1735).

141a (*above*) Upminster Church interior with oil lamps typical of the day, *c*.1915.

141b (*left*) Brass with arms of Barnacke, *c*.1500, formerly in Upminster Church but lost since 1861, the rest of the memorial having gone even earlier.

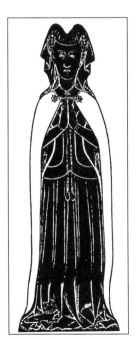
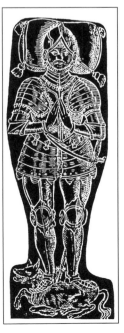

141c (*right*) Brass to Elizabeth Dencourt, *c*.1460. She wears a highly developed and much ornamented form of the 'horned' head dress which is covered by a kerchief, the hair kept in position by a jewelled band. She is clothed in a long, plain tight-sleeved gown, falling down in ample folds, among which nestles a tiny lap-dog with a belled collar. Above this the lady wears a sideless cote-hardie; and over that again a long over-mantle fastened at the breast by means of a cord. An old record says that Roger Dencourt married this lady who was a daughter of Henry de la Felde, through whom he acquired the estate of Gaynes where he resided. The complementary effigy of Roger was still in the church till the middle of the 19th century when it was said to have been sold to a travelling tinker!

141d (*far right*) Effigy of Geerardt d'Ewes in armour, 1591. The effigy and the inscription survive in the church. However, since October 1791, six shields and three other inscriptions which formed part of this brass have all been lost. Because they were recorded by antiquaries like Holman and Weever we do have some records of what has been lost and some historical reconstruction is possible.

142 Upminster Hall, *c.*1920. This is the oldest part—the Hall section dates from the days of Henry VI at which time it was the country seat of the Abbots of Waltham Abbey. The old chapel where the abbots worshipped was taken down in the mid-18th century by Champion Branfill, and the baptismal font was given to St Lawrence's parish church. Near this chapel was a monk's graveyard. The Branfills were associated with the hall as lords of the manor from the time it was purchased by Andrew in 1685 till the last Branfill, Colonel Benjamin Aylett Branfill, emigrated to New Zealand in 1881. Andrew, the first Branfill at the Hall, had been captain of a ship at the age of 19; later with his own ship *Champion* he built up a fortune and reached 40 as a rich widower. In 1681 he married his second wife Damaris Aylett of Kelvedon Hatch—and so both Champion and Aylett, names which have ever since been associated with the Branfills and Upminster, began with Andrew. The hall is now owned by Upminster Golf Club.

143 (*above*) Gaines or Gaynes—this view of about 1916 shows the latter version built by the Rev. George Clayton in 1846. After his death his widow married Henry Joslin. She died in 1873. The house was demolished after Joslin's death in 1927 and sold for development. The site was originally that of the lords of Gaynes Manor, especially the Engaynes and the Deyncourts. Sir James Esdaile, who came and changed the face of the manor and village by reconstructing most of the subsidiary houses, also built the most substantial mansion ever known in the parish. Unfortunately very little record of it remains and it predates the age of photography, lasting from 1771 to 1820, although a final eastern portion was taken down in 1845 by Thomas Wilson, father of the historian.

144 Upminster village map of 1897—a mine of information about the village at this date, before the tide of development swept across its feudal acres.

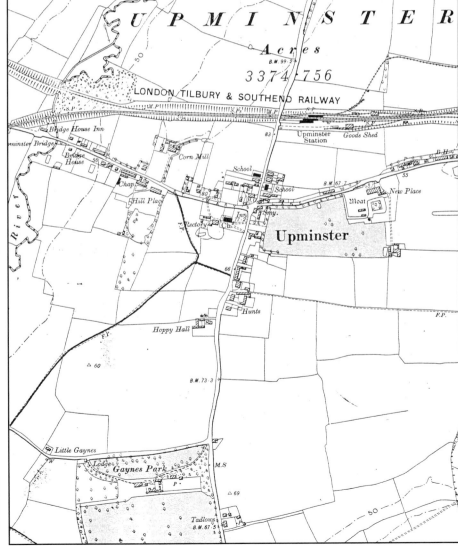

145 Upminster's smart firefighters at the fire station, 1910. In 1909 they were said to be enlisted. The appliances were stored with Capt. Hutson. In 1908 nearly £58 was spent on purchasing the best Southwark brand hose with brass ends on each length. However, their work record appears to be less efficient than their appearance. Although they dealt with smaller blazes such as one in an elm tree, the Hornchurch brigade had to be called to two important fires, one at Gaynes Park, and a later one at Martins Farm, Hall Lane. The Upminster hoses were not able to get a supply from a nearby pond and by the time the Hornchurch brigade arrived the farm was gutted. This kind of problem continued until amalgamation in 1935.

146 Above Upminster station in 1905. This slightly damaged photograph shows part of the village on the eve of development. Can the man be the ubiquitous T.L. Wilson again? The hoarding is probably advertising land for sale.

The Real Garden Suburb.

Only 15 miles from the City.

UPMINSTER

Particulars, Plan & Conditions of Sale

70 CHOICE PLOTS OF FREEHOLD LAND

ON THE

CRANHAM PARK ESTATE.

To be Sold by Auction

On WHIT-MONDAY, JUNE 8th, 1908,

In a marquee on the Estate, at 2.30 o'clock p.m.

THE LAND COY., 68 Cheapside, London, E.C.

147 Prospectus for the Cranham Park Estate (Moor Lane, Cranham Gardens, The Crescent, Queen's Gardens, King's Gardens), 8 June 1908.

148 Hall Lane, *c*.1913.

149 Ashburnham Gardens, 1913.

150 Cranbourne Gardens, 1920.

151 Deyncourt Gardens under construction.

152   Courtenay Gardens, 1910.

153   Gaynes Road, 1920.

154 Waldegrave Gardens, 1913.

155 Looking across the wide open spaces to Station Road and the site for the Congregational church, 1910. Roomes Stores also now stands on this Station Road frontage.

UPMINSTER, Essex.

Three miles from Romford, on the main line to Southend-on-Sea (Midland Railway, L. T. & S. Section), and under forty minutes to London.

THE VALUABLE FREEHOLD PROPERTY

KNOWN AS THE

Upminster Estate

Beautifully Timbered, extending to an area of about

478 Acres

and having an actual and estimated Rent Roll of

per **£1306 16s. 0d.** *ann.*

Comprising the Agricultural Lands, known as

CHAPMAN'S FARM and FARM HOUSE.   **UPMINSTER HALL FARM.**
MARTIN'S FARM.   **GREAT WILCOCKS.**

About 66 ACRES immediately on the West of UPMINSTER GARDEN ESTATE.

A considerable portion being ripe for

BUILDING DEVELOPMENT.

The Brickfield and Premises with Sixteen Cottages let to the New Upminster Brick Works, Ltd. Several Excellent **FREEHOLD GROUND RENTS** in the centre of Upminster Village, secured upon Shop, Stables, Buildings and Four Houses.

The Freehold Residence known as "America Lodge,"
and **BUILDING LAND.**

The Lordship of the Manor of Upminster Hall,
Including TYLER'S COMMON and certain Manorial Wastes, with Quit Rents and other Dues.

To be offered for Sale by Auction in LOTS (unless sold previously by Private Treaty), by Messrs.

YATES & YATES

At Winchester House, Old Broad Street, E.C.,

On THURSDAY, JANUARY 20th, 1921, at 2.30 o'clock precisely.

Particulars and Conditions of Sale can be obtained of the Solicitors: Messrs. CLARKE, CLARKE & SQUARE, 28, Bolton Street, Piccadilly, W.1.; or from the Auctioneers' Offices:

Telephone: MAYFAIR 501 (Two Lines).   **12a, HANOVER SQUARE, W.1.**

R.O. D658.

---

156 Upminster Estate sale brochure, 1921. This sale could have led to an extensive urbanisation of the open areas north of the station. Fortunately development was slower than expected, and much land remained as open fields.

157 Looking from Hall Lane north across the Southend Road to Hall Lane South on 26 April 1928. This recently built road undoubtedly made a strong impact, giving a further boost to Upminster's development. In the light of today's traffic it seems strange that you could cut across Southend Road on the level in 1928.

158 The presence of a policeman at Upminster crossroads, *c*.1929, seems to indicate that traffic was becoming a problem.

159 The Capitol cinema, opened in St Mary's Lane in 1929. Upminster folk now no longer needed to travel beyond their village to see the latest film.

160 Crumpled Horn Dairy and Tea Garden, 1926. The Upminster Garden Suburb prospectus describes Upminster as an 'Essex Beauty Spot'. This was no doubt enhanced by the creation of this place of refreshment.

161 The Upminster Garden Suburb estate office faced the station. Motor cars were parked ready to convey interested parties to view the new homes and amenities of the estate.

162 Bungalows in St Mary's Lane, Cranham, *c*.1925.

UPMINSTER

CRANSTON PARK ESTATE

CRANSTON PARK
ESTATE
UPMINSTER

With the Compliments of

A. E. PALMER

ESTATE DEVELOPER

CORBETS TEY ROAD
UPMINSTER, Essex.

Telephones : Upminster 328
Private : Billericay 104

163 The Cranston Park Estate developed by A.E. Palmer included Park Drive, Cranston Park Avenue, Melstock Avenue, Brackendale Gardens and Coniston Avenue, 1931.

164 Development in Front Lane, Cranham, 1930s.

165 Rectory Gardens, Cranham—a peaceful scene, 1930s.

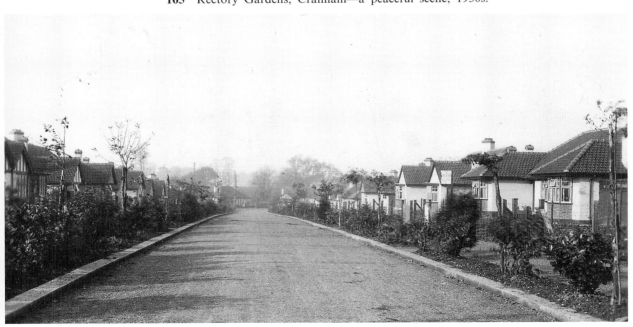

166 Upminster from the air, 28 October 1938, showing its suburban acres and the railway line at the bottom.

167 Moor Lane, 1938. The only car in the avenue—peace and quiet, near the shop, on the verge of the fields, what's on at the cinema (Capitol and the Towers) ... what more could a person want?

168 Roomes Stores in the 1930s was the place to go. Since its opening in 1927 this Upminster store has attracted many visitors to the centre. The café and restaurant advertised here and the specialised departments make Upminster that little bit different from everywhere else for shopping.

VISIT The CAFE RESTAURANT

Popular Price Luncheons
SUMMER TIME MENU
SOMETHING DIFFERENT EVERY DAY

See the Windows
AT
The MAN'S SHOP
Opposite
THE STATION

ROOMES STORES L^TD.
THE SUNNY SIDE OF STATION ROAD
UPMINSTER

STORE OPEN
to 5 p.m.
THURSDAY
1 o'clock

Index

Roman numerals refer to pages of narrative text, and arabic numerals to individual illustrations.

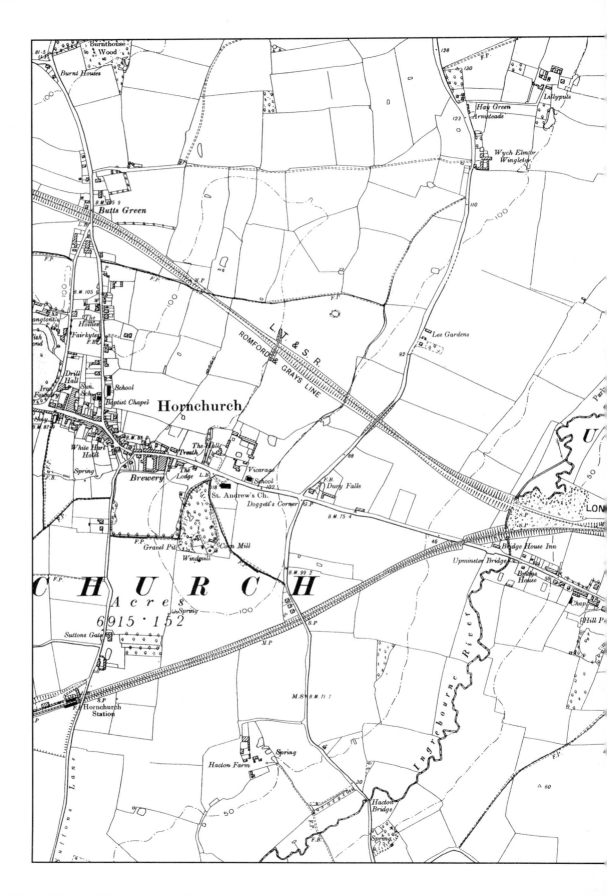